Birkenhead

Priory

by

Jean McInniss

For my dear friend
and Godmother "Bow",
(Mrs Gertrude Catherine Wright).

First published 1983 by Countyvise Limited, 1 & 3 Grove Road, Rock
Ferry, Birkenhead, Wirral, Merseyside L42 3XS.

ISBN 0 907768 15 6

Copyright © Jean McInniss, 1983
Photoset and printed by Birkenhead Press Limited, 1 & 3 Grove Road,
Rock Ferry, Birkenhead, Wirral, Merseyside, L42 3XS.

CONTENTS

Fig. 2: A reproduction of a pencil drawing by David O'Connor of the Crypt looking west. (Sometimes called the sub-vault or undercroft.)

THE GUIDED TOUR

The old stones of the Priory looked down with the stoicism of great age. Yet another group of the current generation filled with a sense of their own importance were passing through. They were only temporarily the inheritors of these walls just as all the past generations had been. The ruins remembered them all, right back from the founder, Hamo de Mascy, grandson of one of William the Conqueror's nobles. — What an attractive man King Edward I had been with his tall form, and shoulder-length hair and clipped beard. 'Longshanks' they had called him. Tents and pavilions had been erected outside for his retinue during that last visit in 1277 — and all those horses! The bill for feeding them had been colossal. . . . . Then there had been Henry VIII's royal bailiff, Randle Arrowsmith, who had helped dismiss the monks in that distant year, 1536. Oh what sadness, what unspoken anxiety there had been when the monks had been told that they would have to leave their home. All that they had tried to do was to worship God and serve their fellow men — just as the commandment said. The Priory remembered Ralph Worsley who had taken over and later the Powell family through many generations. Later still had come the Prices, one of whom had rebuilt the exterior house which had been dismantled by the Parliamentarians in the Civil War. But the destructors of Cromwell's day had not been the only destroyers. Later vandals had ruined this beautiful headland of birch and oak trees and the clean sands of the river with great ugly shipyards and docks and had brought countless folk to that formerly quiet spot. It was they who had built St. Mary's Church, the shell of which remained as a neighbour. How proud they had been of those cast-iron window traceries, such a symbol of their industrial revolution. Without the spire of St. Mary's, the Priory's site would have disappeared from view behind the sprawling industrialization. St. Mary's had come and gone over a short while, the Priory reflected, remembering the long-skirted women folk with their bonnets and shawls and the bewhiskered gentlemen who had looked so prosperous and sure of themselves as they had desecrated what was left of the Priory in the name of 19th century industrial progress. Yes, the people of all those generations, though looking different from this group of casually dressed modern people had also thought of themselves as the inheritors though the ruins had known that they too would soon be dust. For a time the town's nobility had been the Priory's neighbours, but this last hundred years, what decay, what slums, what desolation had surrounded it. Factories, flats and houses had come and gone leaving dereliction and vandalism every bit as soul-less as that of Cromwell's day. The Priory could scarcely recall now the beauty of its former setting, the daisy-strewn meadows ripe with buttercups, the clean and fresh river, the wide sandy expanse and the rocky inlets of its promontory. These folk, as they stood there looking about them with eyes of interest, could have no idea what it, the Priory, had once been as it stood on its beautiful peninsula surrounded on three sides by water, a headland of oak and birch and meadow crowned with red sandstone.

. . . . . .

The group of visitors were crossing the remains of the cloister garth. The guide was telling them that there would have been a covered walk all around the garth which would have connected the various buildings. They had now gone into the undercroft (Fig. 2) — unspoilt — of course those lamps were an addition. There was a quern for grinding flour over there. The guide supposed it had been a cellar for storage — nice and cool for wines and food. Notice the floor — rough beaten earth, rock and rubble. The monks had gone to immense care to tile the church but for themselves they'd been content with the natural rough surface of the site. The kitchen was thought to have been through that way. No trace of it now. The party began to ascend the twisting staircase. The refectory or frater (Fig. 3) as it was called, had been up above. Yes — odd

Fig. 3: 'Refectory area' looking east. Present walling is largely post-suppression.

Fig. 4: The Guest Hall and Prior's apartments. Western range facing south. (From a pen and ink drawing by David O'Connor.)

to have it upstairs — more work and the business of keeping food warm. The pottery had been green and brown. Meal for porridge had been prepared in two large stone mortars. The Priory had had its own fish ponds.

Our monks had earned their living by being ferrymen and farmers. The care of ferries and roads and bridges was a very important service. Liverpool had been founded in 1207. Traffic across the river was increasing by the end of the 13th century. The boat must have been an awkward craft to handle, very cumbersome — when you think it had to carry horses and sacks of corn and probably livestock as well as laden passengers going to and from market. The crossing depended on the wind and tide. If the weather was very bad travellers had to put up at the Priory. That's why the Prior petitioned for permission to build a hostel and to make a charge for food. Even if one believed that each traveller might be Christ Himself in disguise, feeding a constant stream of people must have been a strain on resources. The same with the ferry — the monks had looked on this service as a pious duty — an act of charity. Maybe the better-off passengers had given voluntary gifts. But in the end the monks had asked if they might charge tolls. — There's a tapestry in the Williamson Art Gallery showing the Prior receiving the Charter, granting the special ferry rights, from Edward III. — If the boat was required over in Liverpool the signal was a lighted beacon on the shore.

The monks' farm was on a sort of plateau up where Alfred Road is today. The Prior was like a manorial lord with tenants and serfs. There were usually about six lay stewards or bailiffs but they had a co-operative method of working together. We know a chap called Richard, the son of a Claughton carter called William, stole some of the Priory cattle. The Prior got them back. He not only forgave Richard, he let him go on working for him. There's a story about another Richard from Claughton — name of Hiccock. He fell from a scaffold when he was working at the Priory in 1523. He 'broke his head!'

Hospitality was one of the main tenets of the Black Monks.

There were a lot of pilgrims about in those days. Folk might be travelling to St. Werburgh's shrine in Chester. Other pilgrims would be going over to Hilbre Island carrying their scallop shell as pilgrim's token or badge. Long before the Priory, a holy woman called Hildeburgh had lived on the island. It's called after her. We think it was one large island in those days. The monks from Chester set up a cell there for Retreats. They built a chapel in honour of Our Lady which brought in even more folk from far and wide.

The guide had now conducted the party into the west wing. This had been the guest hall (Fig. 4) for the more important guests. Over there it was the Prior's lodging. The monks' parlour had been under his room. 'Must have had a very low-ceiling! At midnight one summer night in 1509, a Tranmere labourer called Nicholas Barbar broke into the Prior's room and stole his ring. A Chester court sentenced him to be hanged.

Lawless men operated in those days too. Once the Prior's boat had been stolen. There'd been a case in 1402 of the ferryman being wounded by robbers who'd hidden in the trees waiting for the arrival of the laden boat so they could beat up and rob the passengers.

"I'm trying to imagine it all," one of the ladies exclaimed as she examined masons' marks in the stone. "It's strange to think of them all living here hundreds of years before we were born."

The Priory recalled the Benedictine monks in their black habits. There'd been so many of them in four hundred years but only maybe sixteen at a time. They'd peaceably occupied its buildings, living quiet, blameless and thus unreported lives. Why, even Henry VIII's commissioners had been quite unable to find proof of any wrong-doing no matter how hard they tried. Of course that little matter in 1340 of the Prior knowingly receiving John de Stabulo and sharing in his spoils of venison had long been forgotten. The Priory thought of

9

them with a keen and tender regret wishing that by some miracle they might be restored and these strangers vanish as the ghosts that they really were. It was the Benedictine monks who were real to the Priory. These modern folk didn't belong. They lacked understanding for all the patient interest in their eyes. Of course it had been such as these who had tried to restore the ravages of wanton destruction and of time. At least that wretched ivy had been removed, as were those sycamores growing in the guest hall floor. But the Priory had a special secret all of its own. The monks had been back! After all of these hundreds of years Benedictines had crossed its precinct and had been in the Chapter House. It had happened after the 1500th anniversary of St. Benedict's birth late in 1980. But the Priory now knew that to this day men were still becoming Benedictine monks, following the same life style as the Priory's inhabitants had once done all that long time ago. The Priory could remember the mystic quality of the 2 a.m. candle-lit procession to the church for Night Office and the solemn ritual of the day-time services. How peaceful and beautiful the monks' singing had been creating a pool of tranquility with occasional deep silences which even the comings and goings of visitors to their church could not disturb.

The visitors were making their way to the Chapter House (Fig. 5). A pity about the cloister. Fancy the Victorians using it as a graveyard — and as for that dry dock over the wall! That dated from 1956; by then people should really have known better! No chance now of excavation on the site of the Priory church. But there had been finds — coins and tiles and pottery. Had they visited the Williamson Museum? And those skeletons they'd found — perfectly preserved — even the teeth. At least one had been a Prior. The stone was on the floor at the east end.

The tourists were absorbing the Chapter House (Fig. 6). "12th century," the guide explained. "Norman — look at the

Fig. 5: Front view of Norman Chapter House with Scriptorium over. St. Mary's in background.

Fig. 6: The Chapter House interior looking east.

pillarwork — and the roof. Ribbed. The Chapter House was where the monks met at about half past eight in the morning. It was a time for discussing business and for handing out punishments! You know, if a monk had been late for church — if he'd overslept or broken the Rule in some way — he'd have to say extra prayers or go without his supper! The Chapter House was used as a chapel after the dissolution. We know there was a curate here in 1635. He was the Reverend Charles Adams and he's recorded as paying Charles 1st Ship Money tax. It was reconsecrated earlier this century. After St. Mary's was demolished it took over as the Parish Church. It's the oldest part of the Priory — beautifully preserved — a gem.

"How dreadful it must have been for the monks when the Priory was closed down. It must have been far worse than being made redundant. They lost their home as well. Their whole way of life had to change."

"It's said they were given 40/- each and a new gown. The Prior surrendered so he didn't share the fate of the Prior from Norton who's supposed to have been hanged outside his Priory.[1] The smaller houses were the first to go. The Priors faced death or imprisonment if they gave the King's Commissioners any trouble. Our Prior not only successfully avoided any unpleasantness, he got himself a decent pension into the bargain.[2] What happened to them afterwards is anyone's guess. They may have made their way to Chester. St. Werburgh's didn't close until 1541. Perhaps they earned a living singing in local churches and, don't forget, they were experienced farmers and ferrymen. They could probably do a hand's turn at wood-carving and book-binding as well. Anyway, a historian called Leland, who visited the Priory some years after the dissolution, wrote that he'd found it deserted. How sad the old place must have been."

The guide led the party past the Laird vault and up a rickety iron staircase. "Yes, that's where John Laird was buried. Canon Andrew Knox was the vicar of St. Mary's round about that time."

Fig. 7: The 'Scriptorium', a room added above the Chapter House in the 14th century.

The visitors were now looking around the large room which had been built up above the Chapter House. "It's called the Scriptorium (Fig. 7). We don't really know what it was used for, any more than we know the precise site of the monks' ferry. 'Still contains lockers for books and writing materials."

The voices had been rising and falling for some time — in cadences of sound and silence. The group now began to disperse. They faded away from the Priory. It knew from long experience that there would be others to take their place. Silence settled. Particles of dust shone in the air. The river, its old neighbour, monotonously flowed past, no longer beautiful and now spoilt by the pollution of 'progress'. The Priory settled down into its familiar dream of recapturing the faces from the past. They were all there — part of its being. The founder — had he secured eternal salvation for himself? That handsome king and his retinue. Generation after generation of travellers bent on crossing the river, sometimes seeking hospitality for days at a time — and then there were the earnest Victorians and countless people, some of whom had looked dirty and pinched and poor. As for the monks — a blur of faces from those 400 years — the jolly ones, the courteous, the otherworldly and devout, the scholarly and ascetic, young growing old — the Priory knew that in spirit they were still there to support it in its lonely sojourn in this alien century. But was it so alien? The Priory had its secret joy. It knew that the Benedictine monks were back. The sun broke through and warmed the old sandstone walls which had withstood the sieges and enmity of men and the ravages of centuries. It had not existed in vain. What it had stood for would last as long as time itself.

---

[1] Norton and a Convent in Chester were suppressed at the same time. An arch from the Convent, St. Mary's, a Benedictine nunnery founded in 1140, was re-erected in Grosvenor Park, Chester.

[2] £12 per annum which he would lose if he obtained another position.

Fig. 8 : Sixteen-tile 'composition' as most probably appearing at Birkenhead Priory, also at St. Mary's Nunnery in Chester. (By courtesy of Mrs. E.H. Brotherton-Ratcliffe).

Fig. 9: 14th century 'line-impressed' tiles. Top right is the only one not found among Priory tiles but probably was there originally. (By courtesy of Mrs E.H. Brotherton-Ratcliffe).

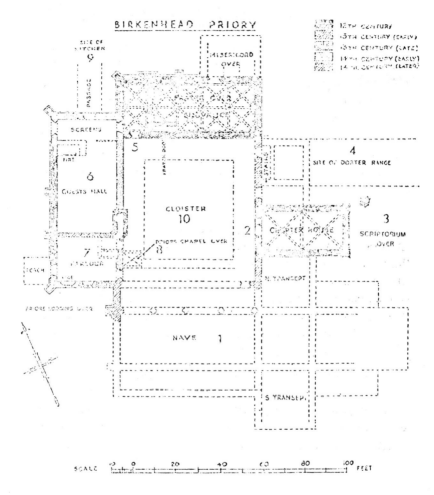

Fig. 10: A plan of the Priory layout as issued by Birkenhead
Corporation in their short guide to the Buildings.

1. The PRIORY SITE and buildings

Wirral was once the Earl of Chester's hunting forest, one of the three great forests of Cheshire. (The others were at Delamere and Macclesfield.) Before the advent of the Normans, Wirral had been an area of natural woodland and open spaces with farms and cottages which the new overlords levelled so that their pursuit of game could flourish.[1] Wild boar and wolves lurked in Storeton and Bidston woods. Traces of woodland still exist in these districts and also at Eastham and Burton.

There was a track through the forest from Chester which wound its way along a route which today we would call Old Chester Road, Holt Hill, Whetstone Lane and the Grange Precinct, to where the Mersey was about half a mile wide and the best place to cross. Here the Priory was built on a rock of red sandstone washed by the river. To the south was Tranmere Pool, and to the north, Wallasey Pool, then thought to have been a mile wide at its mouth. The track formed the landward side of what must have been a very pleasant Priory 'peninsula'.[2]

At low tide there was a short-cut across Tranmere Pool. Stepping stones led over the sandy expanse to the neighbourhood of the Priory. Care had to be taken as to just when to cross — (as in making one's way to Hilbre Island today.) There were reports of travellers being drowned.[3]

Birkenhead Priory would have been enclosed, as other contemporary monastic houses, by a wall or ditch with a gateway. The buildings were in the south-west angle of the site, which was on high ground at the end of a promontory[4] (Fig 11).

The ground plan (Fig. 10) was not the usual one. The cloisters were to the north of the church, as at Chester. One theory for this is that they were thereby protected from the

18

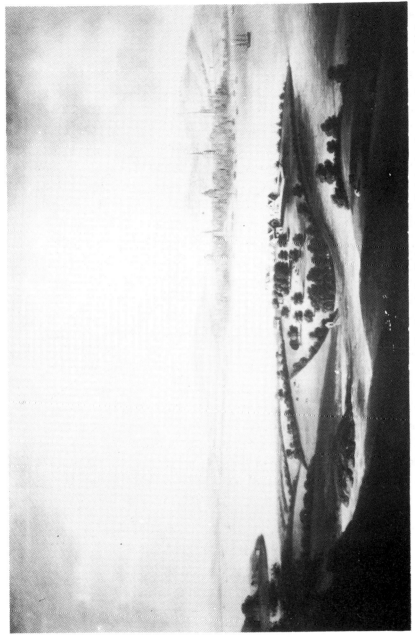

Fig.11: View from Holt Hill overlooking Tranmere Pool and the Priory. An oil painting by an unknown artist probably c1769.

strong south-east and south-west winds. Alternatively, the church was protected by the other buildings from gales sweeping up the river.

A dry dock now occupies much of the site of the Priory graveyard which was used for 800 years. It was the town's principal cemetery as Birkenhead grew until 1864 when Flaybrick Hill came into use. In the mid-nineteenth century interments were taking place at the rate of 500 a year.[5]

The hostel, erected by the 11th Prior, which may have been of timber, was to the south-west of the Priory.[6] Nearby stood the Priory barn, a long stone building, where tithes were accepted and stored. The barn existed as late as 1839. It was blown down by a fierce gale on the night of January 6th in that year.

An old etching of 1728 shows three of the Priory Church's nave pillars still standing (Fig12). When St. Mary's was built, a near neighbour, 1819-22, the remaining north arcading of the 13th century church was sacrificed, and some of the original foundations. The boundary wall of the dry dock, which followed over a 100 years later, marks where the nave would have been.

Benedictine churches tended to be cruciform. It has been estimated that the Priory Church would have had a nave of four bays with north and south transepts, and beyond, the choir and sanctuary. The north aisle of the nave, 9 feet wide, had doors into the cloister at either end. The north transept would have had direct access to the Chapter House, and, after it was built, to the 'Scriptorium' above. The church is thought to have been 120 feet by 52 feet, with the nave being 63 feet long by 27 feet, and the north transept 23 feet by 24 feet from north to south.

Practically nothing at all remains of the church except for a portion of the west wall of the north transept and a portion of the west wall of the north aisle of the nave. At the west end there are the remains of a church buttress and the lower north jamb, (side), of the great west window.

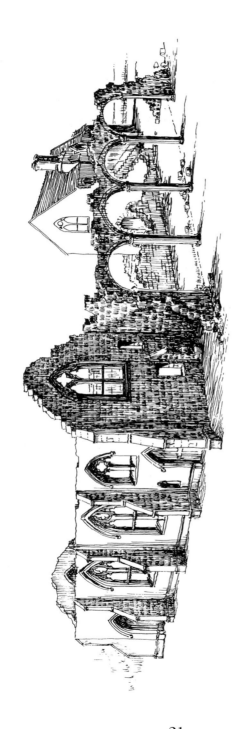

Fig12: Artist's impression, based on an old etching of 1728 when three of the Priory Church's Nave pillars were still standing. The Chapter House with Scriptorium over can be seen in the background. The Priory was at this time in the ownership of John Cleveland. (Illustration : Eric Monks)

Fig. 13: The entrance into the Chapter House. It has a round-headed archway flanked by two small round-headed windows.

Photo: David O'Connor.

The door, which connected the church and the 12th century Chapter House, reverted to being a window, which it had been before the 13th century Priory Church existed.

The entrance into the Chapter House today is via the main door in the cloister area (Fig13). It has a round-headed archway flanked by two small round-headed openings. The Chapter House was one-storey until the room above it was added in the 14th century. It is thought it survived because it was used as a private chapel after the Dissolution. Built in 1150, it is Norman, and the most complete, as well as the oldest, of the Priory buildings. It is 39 feet by 18 feet with one original window (Fig. 14) on the south side at the sanctuary end. There are two late 15th/early 16th-century 5-light windows to the east and north. These broader, traceried, late Gothic windows contrast markedly with the narrow round-arched ones. There is no reason to suppose that they are post-

Fig. 14: Original Norman window on south wall of Chapter House.
(From a pen and ink drawing by David O'Connor.)

23

Fig. 15: Chapter House, Scriptorium over, from North-East. The two late-Gothic windows contrast markedly with the Norman. (From a pen and ink drawing by David O'Connor).

Suppression. The roof is groined, consisting of two squares of quadripartite vaulting. Grooves in one of the pillars show it was once divided by a screen so that it had a vestibule. There is a memorial plaque to Mr. Parry Price on the south side of the east end. When restoration work was taking place, the floor was paved with ancient gravestones, some with medieval inscriptions and motifs, thought to have once covered the graves of priors, monks and local personages. So far only Thomas Rainford's has been identified (Fig. 29).

The original access into the 'Scriptorium' (Fig. 7) was by a flight of steps in the north transept of the church. Today it is via an iron staircase using the same entrance. A later doorway in a corresponding position in the north wall of the room, which led down a flight of steps in the former dorter range, no longer exists. The 'Scriptorium' has a fireplace and original stone cupboards. There is a watching loft which once enabled the monks to see the sanctuary lamp in the church. Repairs took place to this room at the time of the 1st world war. There was damage by incendiary bombs in the blitz in 1941. The roof and the panelling, which were completed at the turn of this century, had to be restored in 1949.

The dorter range, (containing the monks' dormitories), stood to the north of the Chapter House and ran parallel towards the east. There was a rere-dorter to the east or north.[7] Access to the dorter was by means of a doorway in the cloister, (no longer in existence), and stairs leading to a lobby over a passage next to the Chapter House. The passage, still to be seen, may have led to the infirmary over to the east, of which there is no trace.

The cloister would have had alleys around it with windows facing the cloister garth, or centre court. These alleys, containing the carrells, (small study areas), had flat roofs. On the western side the corbels to support the roof remain. The cloister was 66 feet from north to south and 61 feet from east to west.

25

To the north of the cloister there is a range of buildings over a sub-vault, or crypt (Fig. 2). The entrance from this side is via a door leading to steps. The first section of the crypt is smaller than the other section, (two bays as against four bays), and may have been the buttery where provisions were kept. There is a central range of pillars with moulded ribs. Vaulting springs from these octagonal columns without any capitals. In the north-east corner the foundations of a large fireplace can be seen. The north-west corner has a turret staircase. At the summit there are pierced stones for watching purposes.

Above the crypt there are two mid-fourteenth century rooms. Opinion nowadays favours the larger room having been the monks' frater (refectory), and the smaller room to the west of it a guest chamber. However the present walling of this upper stage is largely post-Suppression. The frater could have been gained from the north cloister. A door led into the crypt from where a staircase led up to it. (The walls of this staircase can be seen on the south wall of the crypt.)

On the upper floor there may have been a small apartment known as a misericord. Here special treats, such as meat for sick monks, could have been obtained. The whole of this block may have had a timber roof.

The Western Range, (Fig. 17) dating from the 13th century, is the building nearest to the road. On the outer side you can see the cornice of head and ball-flower ornaments. The almonary window and the porter's window would have been in the western block. The doorway at the southern end was made much smaller in the late 14th century when a two-storied wooden porch was added. The western range underwent much alteration. Many of the surviving features are of a later medieval date.

The whole of this block is 75 feet by 28 feet and contains many interesting windows (Fig. 4). To the north it was a one-storeyed guest hall catering for the more prestigious visitors. To the south it was in two storeys, being the monks' parlour

26

Fig. 16: The original stone cupboards in the Scriptorium.
(From a pen and ink drawing by David O'Connor).

Fig. 17 : The main entrance into the Guest Hall from the roadway. The Western range dates from the 13th century. On the outer side there is a cornice of head and ball-flower ornaments.

with the Prior's apartment over. The monks' parlour, a low square room, was about 20 feet wide and served as an entrance to the cloister. It had a fireplace, window seats, and an obliquely pointed window which would have overlooked the front of the church. There is also a narrow corridor cn the cloister side conjectured to have been used for confessional purposes. The Prior's room was lofty. It had a fireplace. A small spiral staircase was in the angle of the building. The Prior probably had direct access to the church, his own chapel, adjoined his room, being over the flat roof of the cloister alley.

At the opposite end of the western range the guest hall had a lobby formed by a screen. The stone kerb of the hearth protrudes being at right angles to the west wall. This lobby could have been the serving area. It is thought to have had an upper floor with a doorway into the guest chamber above the crypt. A door on the ground floor leads to the crypt. A passage in the centre of the lobby led off in a northerly direction to what is thought to have been a wooden kitchen.

---

[1] Strict Forestry Laws were introduced. The Master Forester lived at Storeton. He would ride through the Wirral with his serjeants. Priors seem to have fallen foul of the law on occasions as when in 1288 the then Prior was called to account for failing to have the claws of his two dogs mutilated. (This was to prevent them attacking game.) Priors appear to have had to make frequent visits to Chester to defend themselves on various charges of this sort. Later a Forester, or one of his serjeants, was billeted at the Priory, which state of affairs lasted until Wirral was disafforested in 1376 by the then Earl of Chester, the Black Prince. (The Black Prince was the son of Edward III, the King who granted the Priory the ferry rights.)

[2] When Edward I was on a visit to the Priory, he gave his permission for this ancient highway to be diverted. It ran through the middle of an open court and must have interfered with the monks' privacy. It was agreed that it should be enclosed within a ditch and hedge or wall. Years later, this was the subject of a complaint by forestry officers.

[3] In 1790 a new turnpike road was built across the mouth of Tranmere Pool. New Chester Road was built on an embankment. It is obvious that the land between the Priory ruins and the upper reaches of Green Lane is low-lying.

Fig. 18: Small obliquely pointing window which would have overlooked entrance to the Priory Church. The formei fireplace above would have been in the Prior's apartment. The former fireplace below would have been in the monks' parlour.

(Photo: David O'Connor).

[4] There is a small drawing of the Priory, in the engraver, Daniel King's, 'Vale Royal' of 1656. The "Vale Royal of England" was reprinted in George Ormerod's "History of Co. Palatine and City of Chester". 1819.

[5] A list, dated 1976, giving over 200 inscriptions from gravestones once in the Priory/St. Mary's Church vicinity is at the Williamson Art Gallery and Museum also a chart showing former positioning.

[6] In the reign of Charles I, Sir Thomas Powell built himself a house, which he called 'The Priory', on the site of the former hostel. When the Civil War was being fought, the Cavaliers' Colonel, Sir Thomas Tyldesley, fortified the house. Troops were all around in the woods. Sir William Brereton took it for Parliament. The Roundheads quartered their horses in the Priory. Eventually the house was rebuilt by the then owner, Mr. Parry Price. At various times in its history it went by other names — Birkett House and Birkenhead Hall, and served as a farmhouse, a boarding school — (achieving notoriety when a young lady managed to slip out and elope to Gretna Green!) — a temporary chapel and as a lodging house. It was finally demolished in 1843. Stones from it, or from the monks' tithes barn, were used for building cottages in White Street, now no more.

[7] The monks' "bathroom".

Fig. 19: Chapter House groining.

2.   BIRKENHEAD and ST. BENEDICT.

The Birkenhead monks belonged to the Benedictine Order. Saint Benedict was born in Nursia in the Kingdom of Spoletto. It was about 70 miles north of Rome. The year was 480 A.D. Four centuries had passed since Christ.

Although he had lived for a time as a hermit in a cave, (the name 'monk' means 'solitary',) Benedict's inner light told him that his vocation was to serve God more actively. He invited other monks to join with him in a community. The monastery he founded was composed of simple huts.

The life established by St. Benedict was one of prayer and self-discipline and hard work. The monks had to support themselves as well as devoting their lives to good works.

Benedict wrote a Rule for his monks. The Rule is really a set of rules. It covers every aspect of the monks' life from prayer and work and study to mundane matters such as clothing, when and what to eat, and when to retire to bed. The monks' day was to be centred around the Divine Office which was sung or recited in choir at intervals during the day. The services of the church are known as the Canonical Hours of the Breviary.

Manuscripts of Benedict's Rule survived the Barbarian invasions being carried by refugees to other monasteries in Rome and in the north of Italy and in Gaul (France). Although other abbots had written a Rule for their brethren, St. Benedict's Rule was the one to gain prominence in the Western world and to survive. This says much for its inherent wisdom and organization. Its survival is also due to the influence of Charlemagne, (Charles the Great, the King of the Franks who lived from 742-814). He had been crowned Emperor of the West by the Pope. Life in each Benedictine Monastery, regardless of country, was similar. Local conditions might bring about slight variations. Each monastery was a family ruled by the Abbot, with its own noviciate for those who wanted to take the vows of poverty, chastity and obedience.

Pope Gregory 1, who was Pope from 590 to 604, was full of missionary zeal. A Benedictine himself, he sent Saint Augustine (destined to be the first Archbishop of Canterbury), to England. A year later and the Benedictine monastery at Canterbury was founded in 597. The Order spread rapidly in England. Until 1100 the only English monasteries, with the exception of early Celtic ones, were Benedictine. In the 13th century there were 40 Benedictine monks at Chester and 16 at Birkenhead Priory, which had been originally colonised from Chester. We know there were only five monks at Birkenhead in 1381 following the Black Death of 1350. In 1535 there were 163 abbeys and priories of the Benedictine Order. All the Cathedral priories, with the exception of Carlisle, belonged to it.

Gradually many different Orders of Religious, that is monks and friars and nuns, besides the Benedictines, came into being. Some are enclosed, that is contemplative, spending their lives in their monasteries praying for the world, others are in 'active' Orders. Monks in very strict Orders are called Trappists.[1] (There was a Cistercian Abbey at Stanlow, and an Augustinian Priory at Norton near Runcorn.)

After Henry VIII dissolved the monasteries, three centuries were to pass before they started to reappear in England. Belmont was established in the mid-nineteenth century, and Downside and Ampleforth at the end of the century. Douai, later to come to England, was in France. In the meantime monks of the English Congregation of Benedictines had managed to keep the continuity and pass on their inheritance on the continent. There are twenty-one Benedictine Congregations altogether.

Twentieth century Benedictines wear the same style of clothing, called a habit, as did their medieval brethren. It is black, which gave rise to the name the Black Monks. They take the same vows and say the same prayers as monks in earlier centuries. Today they run schools and look after Mass Centres and small parishes. Prinknash in Gloucestershire trades in pottery. Buckfast trades in tonic wine. Normally a choir monk, after studying philosophy for 2 years and theology for 4 years, is ordained a priest. Some monks are lay monks like Saint Benedict himself.

Benedictines have always performed valuable services. They have to support themselves. As at Birkenhead they had to establish farmsteads. They would dig and drain the land and clear forests. They cared for travellers, as at our Priory, and to this day, when travelling is no longer so dangerous and such a lengthy and arduous business, they offer hospitality. They also cared for the poor people and for the sick.

The monasteries were centres of learning and the natural home for a scholar. In the days before printing presses, the monks made parchment and ink and paints and laboriously copied books and manuscripts of the ancient world. They illustrated these 'illuminated manuscripts' and decorated the pages with gold leaf. They were artists as well as scholars and their work that has survived is our priceless heritage. The Benedictine inspiration has left us with many wonderful medieval cathedrals and ruins of poignant beauty.

The monks' day was divided into three main areas. There were all the church services. There was the work of the cloister, and the business of providing for the monks' daily needs.

The church services were — Vigils, then Matins, Lauds, Prime, in the early morning. — Terce, Sext and Nones, during the hours of daybreak. — Vespers and Compline in the evening. — There was also Night Office. As well as these services Mass would be celebrated.

Fig. 20: Conjectured reconstruction of the Priory Church taken from 'Birkenhead Priory' by Edward W. Cox (1894).

Prime would be at the first hour of the day, 6 a.m. Terce would be at the 3rd hour. Mass would precede or follow it. Sext would be recited at noon, the 6th hour. Nones was at the 9th hour, 3 p.m. Vespers was in the evening, perhaps at dusk. Compline was the last service of the day when the monks would pray for a quiet night and a perfect end. Bedtime was early, at 7 or 8 p.m. Some six hours later at 2 o'clock in the morning the monks would rise from their beds of straw and proceed to the church. Vigils, Matins and Lauds were before daybreak.

The Canonical Hours of the Breviary or Divine Office, the collective name for the eight daytime services, consists of hymns and prayers and readings from the Scriptures.[2] Over twenty psalms were sung or recited each day so that the whole psalter was completed in a week. The church's calendar, (feast days, religious festivals, etc.,) would influence the services.

The monks must have found the unheated church very cold, especially in the mid-winter. Except for nights of the full moon it must have been inky black, lit only by the glow from the candles. They would have slept ready dressed although they would have removed the belt which contained their knife. (Each monk had possession of a knife and a needle). A light was kept burning in their dormitories. There would be ten or twenty beds.[3] Their clothing, of coarse cloth and hooded, was of the simplest kind. Each monk had two suits. The top of his head would be shaved. This was called a tonsure.

They would probably have had one advantage over the townsfolk. Monastic buildings usually had running water. Benedictines were keen on cleanliness and good sanitary arrangements were considered important.

They did not have forks so washing would tend to follow a meal. They might breakfast simply of bread and porridge or have two meals, one at 11 a.m. and one at 6 p.m. They would take turns to cook or wait on their brothers. They had a common table and were allowed 1-lb of bread and a little wine.

Fig. 21: Looking south-east towards Priory Church from cloister-garth. Conjectured reconstruction taken from 'Birkenhead Priory' by Edward W. Cox (1894).

There would be milk and eggs. Meat was only allowed in the sick bay but fish would be served on occasions. The monks would sit in silence during the meal listening to one of their number reading from a religious or edifying book in Latin. (An example of a refectory wall pulpit can still be seen in Chester Cathedral.)

If the church services were the most important part of the monks' lives then second in importance ranked the work of the cloister. Here reading and writing and private meditation or study would go on. Books would be copied and later bound or a journal or records kept.

But someone had to see to the daily running of the Priory. The food had to be grown and prepared for the refectory table. The monks' grange (*grainge*) had to be farmed. Surplus grain had to be taken to market. The fields had to be marled, that is fertilized with lime. The horses and other animals had to be fed. The river had to be fished for trout and herring and salmon. The ferry had to be manned and the needs of travellers attended to. The sick had to be looked after. Tithes had to be gathered and there might be business involving tenants.

Although the monks' day would appear to have been aesthetically satisfying there was much involvement with the workaday world.

---

[1] Other Orders of monks and friars, etc., include Cistercians, Cluniacs, Carthusians, Augustinians, Franciscans, Dominicans, Carmelites and Jesuits.

[2] The 'Sarum' Breviary of the Middle Ages has undergone various enrichments and new forms throughout the centuries. In 1960 Pope John XXIII arranged for the Breviary to be reorganized and simplified.

[3] Modern monks do not have to rise in the small hours for Night Office. They do get up early, around the same time as workers on an 'early shift'.

Fig. 22: 'Birkenhead Priory Restored' — an impression of how the Priory looked in the 14th century by E. W. Cox.

3. BIRKENHEAD PRIORY
Territories — Possessions — Rights

Birkenhead Priory is thought to have come into being about sixty years after Chester Abbey had been founded by Hugh Lupus. The year 1150 is often cited as a possible foundation date. The 2nd Hamo de Mascy died in 1185. Perhaps it was he or his son who was the founder.[1]

The Priory was for fifteen or sixteen monks of the Benedicitine Order. This number was not always sustained. Following the Black Death in 1348 there were only five monks at Birkenhead. In 1496 there were reported to be only five and in 1518 and 1524 only 7 monks.

The founder of Birkenhead Priory, Hamo de Mascy, was the grandson of his namesake who held Dunham under Hugh Lupus, Earl of Chester, nephew of William the Conqueror.[2] William had encouraged his knights to endow monastic establishments. He himself had endowed Battle Abbey, near Hastings, and Hugh Lupus had endowed Chester Abbey.

Although colonized from Chester, Birkenhead is not thought to have been merely a cell of the larger house. Churches were already established in Wirral. In 1348 a secular priest was appointed to the Priory which would seem to suggest that none of the monks at that time were in priestly orders.

The Priory never sought royal patronage to become an Abbey. One explanation might be that it would have been an insult to the founder's memory and to his family. Sir Hamo de Mascy had founded a *priory*.

Its territory was originally part of the barony of Dunham. The manor of Claughton came with the endowment and all of Birkenhead but not Oxton and Tranmere. In twentieth century terms the boundary ran from the River Mersey to Wallasey Pool, (at that time much nearer), and as far as Poulton bridge.

It then extended to Birkenhead North station and up Flaybrick Hill. It skirted Bidston and Oxton passing near St. Aidan's Terrace on its way to Christ Church, and from there down to Borough Road, once the bed of the Birkett stream which fed into Tranmere Pool, and so to the Mersey again. The land inside this boundary line belonged to the Priory. The Priory mill was thought to have been near to the top of Tranmere Pool, (sometimes called Birkett Pool.) It was here that the stream swelled out at its confluence with the river.

Within this area a Grange or Farm was set up. Hilda Gamlin, a nineteenth century Birkenhead authoress, who lived in Grange Mount, recalled the farm on the same site when writing in 1892. She called it Old Grange Farm and said the boundaries of the farm were Alfred Road — Grange Mount — Euston Grove and Euston Place.[3]

Stones to be found in the boundary walls of houses in upper Alfred Road, near to its junction with Westbourne Road, are reputed to be from the monks' grange or its outbuildings.

Hamo de Mascy, the son and heir of the 4th baron, gave to God, the Blessed Virgin Mary and to Saint James, and to the Prior and Convent of Birkenhead, half an acre of land in Dunham Massey and the advowson of the Church of Our Good Lady, St. Mary, in Bowden. To this day the house on the site of the monks' grange there, (an old vicarage used as a farmhouse), bears the name 'The Priory'. It is nice to think that the surrounding landscape may have changed little in character since in the ownership of the monks.

Bowdon Church has been much rebuilt. It remained a Norman building until the 14th century. It seems possible that the Mascys were buried there. We know that their descendents are.

At least one Prior was buried in the church. Sketches were

made of the tomb and of some of the chantry windows given by Priors, by the Chester Herald, Randle Holme, which are in the Harleian Manuscripts in the British Museum.[4]

The Priory was not thought to have ever been a rich monastic house.[5] Nevertheless it had been given good endowments and over the centuries people left gifts of money and parcels of land to it. There must have been many small bequests such as the following examples from two 16th century Wills:-

In 1527 John Meols left 6/8d to the Priory. This money was to be used for a painting of the 'crucifixion' for the church.

In 1531 George Booth of Dunham Massey gave his best horse to the Prior and asked for his prayers. He also gave 10/- for thirty Requiem Masses for his soul.

Parishes paid tithes for the support of religion which if not given in money were paid in kind — with goods and produce, etc. No compulsory alms were given. No one had given an endowment for the poor. It could be that there were no poor people living in the vicinity.

Birkenhead Priory controlled the hospital of St. John the Baptist which stood outside the North Gate in Chester. This was an alms house of thirteen beds which had been given into the mastership and keeping of the Prior by Edward I. This was later confirmed by Henry III. It had been built on extra parochial land adjacent to the parish of St. Oswald. The following account is in the Harleian Manuscripts, (2159 104):—

> "... that there ought to be, ... in the said hospital three chaplains to say Mass daily, two in the church and the third in the chapel, before the poor and feeble sustained in the hospital, and that one lamp ought to be sustained

at Mass every day in the hospital, and to burn every night in the whole year, and that thirteen beds competently clothed should be sustained in the same hospital, and receive thirteen poor men of the same city, whereof each shall have, for daily allowance, a loaf of bread, a dish of pottage, half a gallon of competent ale, *and a piece of fish or flesh, as the day shall require."*

At a time when there was found to be only six widows in the hospital, presumably not requiring so much ale! — and only one chaplain — the Prior pleaded that the revenues, (which were £4.11/- annually from Randle, the Earl of Chester, paid to the Exchequer, and rents from lands and houses belonging to the hospital), would not suffice to support a larger number.[6]

Birkenhead Priory held the richly endowed rectories of Backford and Bidston and the rectories of Bowdon and Davenham, sharing Wallasey with Chester Abbey, also a good deal of land in these parishes as well as in Moreton, Claughton, Tranmere, Over Bebington and Saughall Massie. There was also the Manor of Davenham; extensive estates in Wallasey; fifteen acres of land in the Manor of West Derby and estates in different parts of Lancashire.

Thirteenth and fourteenth century endowments of land yielded rents or other forms of income. There were parcels of land in Cheshire, Warrington and nearer at hand in Newsham, Smithdown and Wavertree.

The Prior had extensive manorial and feudal rights and the rights of fisheries, wreckage and boats from the manor of Oxton to half way across the Mersey. He had the rights of common for his beasts and those of his tenants at Tranmere. He had pasture rights and the right to dig turf in Bidston, Moreton, Saughall, and the right to hold a court of the Manor of Claughton.

Via Royal Letters Patent from Edward II, dated 1318, and Edward III, dated 1330, the Prior could charge for the accommodation and food received by travellers, and he had the right of ferrying and to charge for the service.[7]

The monks dealt in grain at Liverpool market. It was more convenient than Chester. They rented land for their stall. In 1346 they acquired a granary in Water Street. This tenement had a great pair of stone stairs at the back. The monks stored grain from one Saturday to the next on an upper floor. (In the 17th century it was known as Jonathan Hunter's house.) This burgage site brought with it several of the strips in the town-fields. One of these strips was called 'the Prior's Hey'.

It is conjectured that the monks' ferry house stood at a point where Pool Lane began. This lane led from a point near the mouth of The Pool in a northerly direction to where Derby Square is today.

Until recent times there have been other traces of the monks' existence in Wirral. Down the western slopes of Bidston Hill, beyond the railway bridge, there was a twenty acre field dedicated to St. James. It neighboured Lady Field. These fields, dedicated to its patron saints, may well have been held by the Priory.

Moreton had a Prior's field and a Dove House Yard. Perhaps the monks had a columbarium there. (Pigeon-house.)

When excavation was taking place in connection with Birkenhead docks, traces of an old wooden bridge were found. This bridge was beneath the old line of the roadway from Birkenhead to Bidston. It had been about 100 feet long with oaken beams resting on rock at either side and on intermediate stone piers. It was thought to have once crossed a stream or tributary later converted into the Great Float and filled in. It is possible that it was built by the monks and their helpers.

---

[1] There are variations in the spellings of these names, e.g. Hamon; Masci; Massie; Mascy; Doneham, (etc.)
'Massey' or 'Massie' are most commonly used today.
Other names for Birkenhead Priory are Bircheved, Bucheved, Byrkett, Burket, Birkett, Berket etc.

[2] According to the Domesday Survey, much of the land bestowed upon the Mascys had belonged to a Saxon called Eluard who was dispossessed at the time of the Conquest.
A castle or fortified house was built at Dunham for the family. Unlike Puddington Manor, also held by the first baron, it is not mentioned in the Domesday Book. The district of Dunham, near to Altrincham, is now part of Bowdon. Bowdon Hill, was in a key position being on the main route linking north and south Cheshire. The castle was mentioned in the reign of Henry II. (In 1173 Hamo de Massey held the castle against the forces of the King during a rebellion led by Hugh, Earl of Chester.) It was again mentioned in the reign of Edward II.
For 260 years the Mascys held Dunham Massey in the direct line of descent. The head of the family was always called Hamo. The 6th baron did not have a son. The estates went via the marriage of his daughter, to the Fitton family. After two generations the male line of the Fittons finished. Hamo de Fitton had a daughter who married Richard Venables, the younger son of the Baron of Kinderton. Dulcie Venables became the heiress. In 1409 she married Sir Robert Booth. During all of this period the Benedictine monks were in occupation of Birkenhead Priory. The Booths' line were still at Dunham at the Dissolution.

[3] "Memories or the Chronicles of Birkenhead." — Hilda Gamlin. 1892.

[4] The Harleian Manuscripts were collections made by Robert Harley, Earl of Oxford (1661-1724), and his son, Edward.

[5] At the Dissolution, the revenues of the Priory amounted to £90.13s.
The Ferry House then brought in £4.6.8d. per annum.
78-acres of arable land brought in £6.4s. per annum.

[6] St. John the Baptist Hospital and its Chapel in the custody of the Priory from 1316 until 1341, were destroyed by Cromwell's men. After the Restoration of the Monarchy, the land went to Colonel Roger Whitley who rebuilt the hospital. In 1687 Chester Corporation took over the charity and duties of keeper.

[7] In 1357 the ferry tolls were:-

> Foot passengers, market days $\frac{1}{4}$d.
> Foot passengers, other days $\frac{1}{2}$d.
> Foot passengers, with pack 1d.
> Man and laden horse 2d.
> Man and unladen horse 1d.
> Quarter of corn 1d.

In 1499 the tolls are quoted as being $\frac{1}{2}$d for a man and the same for every animal. One has only to think how prices would alter in inflation-ridden days given a similar period. However — "William Braas prosecuting on behalf of the crown said that the monks' charges were exhorbitant." (Quoted by Geo. Ormerod.)

4. AFTER THE DISSOLUTION

About 8 or 9 years after the monks had been expelled, the Priory was sold to a former tenant, Ralph Worsley. He paid £568.11.6d. down and £2.19.5d. a year. The third son of William Worsley of the Parish of Eccles, near Manchester, he was in his early fifties. His mother came from a family which had taken the name of Birkenhead. His brothers, Arthur and Antony, did not survive.

Ralph was of the same generation as Henry VIII though about eight years older. He lived through six reigns being born in the reign of Richard III and growing to manhood when Henry VII was on the throne. He survived Henry VIII by a quarter of a century living to be an octogenarian.

Henry knew him well. He won the king's approval for good and faithful service. The Charter of 1545 from Henry VIII speaks of Ralph as "our beloved servant", and goes on: —

> "... do give and grant, to the before mentioned Ralph Worseley, all the house and scite of the late Priory of Byrkenhedde, in our County of Chester, suppressed and dissolved by the authority of Parliament, and all the Church Bellfrey and Church Yard of the same late Priory. And all our houses, edificies, mills, barns, stables, dovehouses, orchards, gardens, land and soil whatsoever, as well within as without, and being by or near to the scite, inclosure, compass, circuit, and precinct of the same late Priory. Also all that our messuage and tenement with the appurtenances now or late in the tenure and occupation of Robert Molyneux and one dovehouse, one mill and all the fish yards and 2 acres of meadow and 8 acres of arable land and one parcel of land where flax used to grow. And all the ferry and the ferry house and the boat called the ferry boat and the whole profit of the same with all and singular their appurtenances, situate lying and being in Brykenhedde and Bydeston, and in Kyrekeby Walley, otherwise called

Wallasey, in the said County of Chester, to the said Priory heretofore belonging and appertaining and lately being parcel of the possessions thereof, and being in the proper hands, management, or occupation of the Prior of the same late Priory, at the time of the dissolution of the same late Priory. We do further give, and for the conditions aforesaid, do by these presents grant to the before-mentioned Ralph Worseley the aforesaid house and scite of the said late Priory, and the aforesaid Lordships, manors, messuages, lands, tenements, meadows, feedings, pastures, rents, reversions, services and all and singular other the premises the last Prior had held or enjoyed. . ."

Ralph married and had three daughters who became his co-heiresses. The girls' ages in 1574 — 18 months or so after his death as a very old man — are given as 30; 29 and 28 respectively. Alice, the eldest, married Thomas Powell of Horseley in the County of Denbigh. It was this family who succeeded to the Priory which was held by the Powells for several generations until the line failed in the early 18th century.

Although possessed of the manors of Birkenhead, Claughton and Walton and other territories, Ralph appears to have lived out his life in Chester. He was buried in the church of St. Mary on the Hill neighbouring Chester Castle. It is a 15th century building though the arches of the chancel and the tower are of an earlier date. It is now St. Mary's Centre and run by Cheshire County Council. The marble memorial plaque to Ralph is still to be seen on the east wall of the north aisle though now very worn. There is a flower embossed about half way up. It has a long Latin transcription which in English reads: —

"Beneath this spot is buried the body of Ralph Worsley, Esq., who was the third son of William Worsley of Worsley Meyne, in the County of Lancaster, Esq., and was formerly in the service as Page of the Wardrobe, and one of the stewards of the Chamber of the most mighty

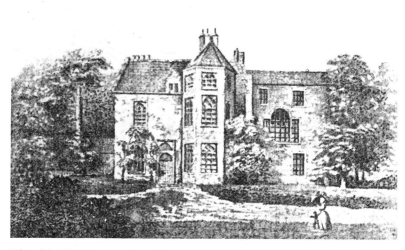

Fig. 23: This house, demolished in 1843, is thought to have stood on the site of the monks' hostel to the south-west of the Priory. It was built by the Price family.

Prince, Henry the Eighth, lately by God's grace, King of England, France and Ireland; to whom the same King on account of the good and faithful service spent about his own Royal person, had out of his Royal bounty given, for the term of his natural life, the offices of Sergeant of the Crown, of Warden of the lions, lionesses and leopards within the tower of London, of Porter of the Great Wardrobe, of controller in the Counties of Chester and Flint, of Clerk of the Crown of Lancaster and of Escheator in the County Palatine of Lancaster, while rewards from other sources were added to these. Pre-eminent mental gifts were bestowed upon him by Heaven, with which he was remarkably endowed, as for example, rare piety towards God, widely-ranging beneficence towards the poor, and wonderful charity towards all men. Having lived more than eighty years, he died on the 27th day of December, in the year of our Lord, 1573, leaving issue, Alice, wife of Thomas Powell, Esq. (who has defrayed the cost hereof), Katherine, married to Thomas Tutchet Esq., and Avice, married to Thomas Vawdrey, gentleman, his children by his wife Joan, daughter of John Pike, Esq.
"By no worldly treasure can heaven be won."

. . . . . .

In 1710, the Priory was bought by a Liverpool merchant, John Cleveland. His daughter, another Alice, who inherited it, also married a Welshman, Francis Price from Flintshire. Like the Powells before them, the Prices owned the Priory in successive generations, for more than 150 years.

In 1890, Charles Aldridge F.R.I.B.A., and E.W. Cox, both members of the Historic Society of Lancashire and Cheshire, appealed for funds to restore the Priory. £3,000 was raised.

The Council acquired the Priory in 1896 and restoration took place the following year, (and again in 1913 and 1973). During the earlier excavations a shaft or cavity was discovered behind the south-west buttress. It measured 1-ft 11-inches by 1-ft 7-inches and stood 10-feet high, 3-feet of this below the surface. All the stones were properly faced inside.

It was during the 1897 excavation that a gold noble from Edward III's reign was found (Fig. 24). The historians thought it could have been put in position for posterity in place of an inscription when the Guest Hall was being built. Also found was an alms token, called a Nuremberg token. This early English Jetton or counter came from one of the Anglo-Gallic mints in France. The design of a heraldic rose, may have been suggested by a badge of Edward I. The token was found outside the almonary window where a wooden shelter for beggars may have stood. It had been dropped 600 years earlier. Like the gold noble, it can be seen at the Williamson Museum.

At the same time fragments of fine tiles were found and medieval earthenware, drinking cups and other utensils and the ruins of an ornamental brick chimney. Elsewhere finely moulded jambs from a window and pieces of window tracery were found. There were corbels (stone supporting projections), with human and animal heads, carved foliage, tracery from a piscina (a stone basin), or sedilia (a stone seat), and fragments of fine mouldings from the church choir or Lady Chapel. Keys were found during renovation work in the Chapter House and nails of the type used in the construction of the Priory (Fig. 25).

The Priory is listed as a building of architectural and historical interest and 1979 was scheduled as an Ancient Monument.

Fig. 24: A gold noble from Edward 111's reign, was discovered during the 1897 excavation.

Fig. 25: Keys found during Chapter House renovation work, and a nail of the type used during the construction of the Priory.

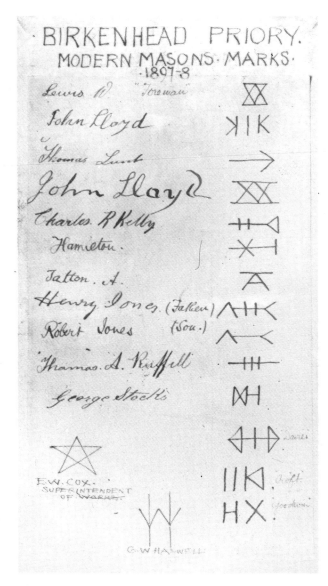

Fig. 26: The names of the stonemasons engaged on restoration work (1897-8) and their marks which can be seen in the stonework today.

Fig. 27: A photograph showing the stonemasons and Priory renovators (1897) which was taken in the Prior's Guest Hall.

Fig. 28: Some medieval gravestones and other stonework assembled during the course of late 19th century restoration work to the Priory.

Fig. 29 : The tombstone of Prior Thomas Rayneford who died in 1473. It was formerly set in the wall to the left of the Chapter House door during the restoration of the Priory but later laid before the altar.

Appendix I
The PRIORS of BIRKENHEAD PRIORY
(+ some Ordinations from the Priory)

According to the Priory Deeds, and as laid down by the Founder, the monks of Birkenhead could choose their own Prior. This was confirmed by Pope Alexander III about ten years after the foundation. The Bishop of Lichfield had to approve the choice. If necessary, he could depose him. It was his job to see no irregularities occurred.[1]

Normal practice was that the lay patron or representative of the Founder would be consulted and a choice made by a few of the monks, or by individual voting, or by unanimous selection.

St. Benedict had laid down that any monk, even one born a serf, could be elected Abbot or Prior. The important thing was that he should be a father to his monks and full of good works and obedient to the will of God. The monks were to choose a good man with the ability to lead them. Once chosen his word was law.

The names of priors are recorded in the Lichfield Episcopal Registers — and elsewhere. They were usually selected from the ranks though on one occasion a monk from Chester was chosen.

The position, one of some standing in the county, was prized by the great families of Cheshire. Though not of the rank of one of the barons, the Prior enjoyed that status. He sat in the Parliament of the Palatinate with families like the Masseys and with ecclesiastics such as the Bishop of Lichfield and the Abbots of Chester, Bangor and Combermere, as well as the Priors of Norton and Stanlow. His name was included as a mark of courtesy with those of county personages as witness to important documents. When he rode out he would be accompanied by his chamberlain and marshal and other officers of his household. He had full feudal jurisdiction over his own domains. The Earl of Chester had released the Prior from 'suit and service' to the court of the Hundred of Wirral. He did not have to pay the customary 8d. fee to the sheriff.[2]

A list of Priors, as far as can be ascertained, would read as follows: —

1190 . . . . . Robert.

1200 . . . . . Ralph.

1206 . . . . . Robert.

1216 . . . . . Oliver. (Witnessed a deed in the reign of King John. i.e. 1199-1216).

1250 - 1283 . . . . . William of Walley (de Waley).

1283 to circa 1300 . . . . . Robert.

1320-2 . . . . . Robert of Bechington. Died 1339?

(?) . . . . . Oliver. (?) Dies 1328. (Note: In 1316 the then Prior was sued by the Vicar of Eastham for seven white loaves and seven bottles of beer of equal competency to that which he used, or, in lieu thereof, to pay half a mark!)

? - Died 1328 . . . . . Robert Millenton or Millington. The Millington family were of Bucklow Hundred. There was a window and monument in Bowdon Church. The monumental slab had the arms of the Millington family and showed an ecclesiastic kneeling and holding in his left hand a cup — (chalice?) On the base his name was inscribed and the date MCCCXXVIII. The window and monument may have been destroyed at the Reformation or during the Commonwealth.

(?) . . . . . Hugh de Aston. He was the second son of Sir Richard Aston. He held office during the reign of Edward III (i.e. 1327-77).

1338-9 - for one year only . . . . . Rober or Robert de Bechington or Becheron.

C.1339 - but resigned immediately . . . . . *James de Neston.* (Jacobus de Neston.)

1339 . . . . .*Henry de Becheton or Bechington.* (Mentioned in 1342 and last mentioned in 1348. He may have fallen victim to the Black Death.)

6th November 1350 to 1357 . . . . . *Thomas de Didsbury.* (Tiddesbury.)

1361-1400 . . . . . *Roger de Tyddesbury.* (He was witness to a stipulation on the part of the Prior of Warrington to found a Chauntry.)[3]

1401 . . . . . *Robert de Honbrugge.* (Robert of Handbridge.) Died 1408.

1408-1425 . . . . . *John Wood or Johane Wode or del Wode.* (On the 20th December 1408, he obtained a dispensation for illegitimacy so he could be elected to any office.) In 1423 he failed to attend a meeting of the General Chapter. The reason given was 'madness'.

1425 . . . . . *Robert de Urmston (Urmeston).* (He did service at Dunham.) He occurs in a Recognizance in £40 dated July 9th 1429 to keep the peace towards Edward Jankyn — his sureties being Sir W. Stanley of Hoton; Sir Thomas Pole; Thomas Hough and John Munshull. Died 1435.

21st June, 1435 . . . . . *Hamon Bostock* - from St. Werburgh's Abbey, Chester, where he had been Prior, that is second in command after the Abbot. He was still Prior in 1439.

1441-1456 . . . . . *Richard Normon.* See "Legends".

C.1456 . . . . . *Hugh Bonor or Hugoni Bover, Hugonis Boner* - also mentioned in 1459. (Is he the same as Thomas Bovere elected in 1455 according to the Lichfield Registers?) Died before 1462.

1462-1473 . . . . . *Thomas Rainford (Reynforth).* (His skeleton was discovered, with two others, in the Priory grounds in the

19th century. The red granite tombstone was first erected on the west wall, left-hand side of the Chapter House door as you enter, but is now at the east end of the Chapter House. (Floor.) A transcription of the wording on his tombstone would be:- "Here lieth Thomas Rayneford, formerly the good vicar of this house who died 20th May in the year of our Lord 1473 on whose soul may God have mercy.)

(?) . . . . . Hugh Gardener - mentioned in and before 1486. (He resigned in favour of his successor.)

1486 . . . . . Thomas Chester (Chestur - other variations). Died 1499.

1499 . . . . . Nicholas Tassy (Stace). (1499 — Nicholas, a monk, elected this year.) Occurs until 1508.

1509 . . . . . Hugh (Hugone) Hyne. Died 1514.

1514 . . . . . John Sharp. (He appears to have been living in 1530 and is thought to have been the last prior before the dissolution in 1536.) He gave a window for Bowdon Parish Church, possibly destroyed at the Reformation or during the Commonwealth. Prior Sharp appears to have been very well regarded by all monks and local gentry.

The steward who took over the Priory premises was Sir Thomas Pole of Pole Hall, Eastham.

. . . . . .

Some Ordinations from the Priory which occur in Lichfield Act Books:-

Randle de Thorald as Deacon September 1310 and 16 October 1316 admitted vicar of Bowdon.

William de Eccleshall as deacon 1314, as priest, 1315.

John de Cestr. as priest 1315.

Samson Goldyng, monk of Birkenhead, as sub-deacon 1419.

Henry Marton, monk of Birkenhead, as sub-deacon 21st May 1429, as deacon 24th September.

Hugh Gregory, Peter Urmeston — monks of Birkenhead, as acolytes[4] 12th March, 1434-5, as priests, 24th September 1440.

Roger Aleyn O.S.B., Birkenhead, as acolyte, 14th March 1488-9; as sub-deacon, 6th March, 1489-90; as deacon, 5th June, 1490.

Richard Rackdale, O.S.B., Birkenhead, as sub-deacon, 23rd September, 1475; as priest, 21st September, 1476.

William Tillesley, O.S.B. Birkenhead, as acolyte, 14th September 1501.

---

[1] The Priory came under the jurisdiction of the See of Coventry and Lichfield there being no Chester bishopric.

[2] Until the 16th century, courts were held at Backford or Willaston every month or so and county freeholders had to travel to them.

[3] A Chauntry or Chantry is an endowment for the singing of Masses.

[4] Acolyte = officer in church attending priest; assistant; novice.

Appendix II
LEGENDS

(1.)

The Story: There was once a boy called Richard Norman. Richard was in the service of a priest. The priest was a member of a religious order. One day the priest accused the boy of some misconduct. Perhaps he had not been doing his work properly. He could have been misbehaving in some way. A heated argument developed. The priest became irate. He snatched up a knife. The boy received a wound. Thinking he was going to be killed the boy drew his own knife. He stabbed his master in the neck. A few days later the priest died from the injury.

The boy was overcome with remorse. He knew he had committed an act of sacrilege. Only the Pope could absolve him. He packed his belongings and began a long and difficult pilgrimage to Rome. He was forgiven for the crime and given absolution. But the boy was unable to forgive himself. He duly performed the penances but decided to spend the rest of his life in prayer and good works. He would become a Benedictine monk. He came to Birkenhead Priory. Here he lived such a good life that he was an example to all. Eventually he was elected Prior.

Fact: A Prior called Richard Normon held the office circa 1440 to 1456.

· · · · · ·

(2.)

The Story: Running from the Priory there were subterranean tunnels. They headed off in various directions. One was said to terminate at the 'red noses', a rocky outcrop off New Brighton. Another ran to Stanlaw (Stanlow) or Ince. A third tunnel led to the nearby river.[1]

The monks, hearing that the Commissioners of Henry VIII were upon them, hurriedly collected together the Priory plate. Two or three of them made off down the tunnel bearing their precious load. The tunnel's entrance was concealed by a large and heavy stone balancing as a door. As the monks gained the passage the stone toppled. It fell onto one monk killing him outright and caused such debris to fall that the remaining unfortunate monks were entombed alive in the passage. Their remains, and that of the Priory plate, has never been recovered.

Fact: There appears to be the beginning of a passageway down in the crypt. It comes to an abrupt end.

. . . . . .

(3.)

A series of events suitable for the plot of a melodrama involved Birkenhead Priory for one of its settings. In 1436, an unfortunate lady called Isabel, the widow of one Sir John Butler of Bewsey in Lancashire, was abducted by William Poole, a member of the family who supplied stewards for the Priory in the 15th and 16th centuries. Despite her protests she was carried off to Bidston Church where she was forced to go through a form of marriage. Later she was discovered incarcerated in Birkenhead Priory by Sir Thomas Stanley.[2]

---

[1] Abbeys and Priories were often well in advance of the towns when it came to sanitation. Underground channels for conducting water and sewage from the buildings could have helped to give rise to the many tales of subterranean tunnels associated with monastic establishments.

[2] In 1361 Roger Lestrange bought the advowson of the priors from the heirs of Hamon de Massey and in 1397 it was sold to John Stanley, an ancestor of the earls of Derby.

Appendix III
The ARMORIAL BEARINGS and the SEAL of Birkenhead Priory

The Priory Arms were taken from those of the Founder, Hamo de Mascy. They were quarterly red and gold. In the first quarter there was a silver lion passant. They were surmounted by a silver crozier, (a pastoral staff or crook), in pale, head turned sinister ways argent. The crozier could have been symbolic of the spiritual authority of the Prior, or the pilgrim staff of the patron saint of the Priory, St. James the Great.[1]

The Priory Seal was of vessica (lozenge) shape.[2] It showed the figure of St. James standing under a Gothic canopy. He wears a pilgrim's hat and cloak and carries a pilgrim's staff in his right hand. In his left hand he holds a book of the gospels across his breast and there is a wallet by his left side. Beneath the saint, under a canopy, is a kneeling figure. This is thought to represent the Founder of the Priory. The groundwork of the seal was filled and fretted with rosettes.

Round the seal in Latin are the words:-

'The common seal of the Priory of St. James of Birkenhead in the County of Chester.'

S.COMMVNE PRIORATVY SCI.JACOBI DE BIRKENEVED IN COM.CESTRI (E).

---

[1] These Arms were taken into the Armorial Bearings for Birkenhead.

[2] There is a rough sketch of the Priory Seal in the Harleian Manuscripts 2074 232. This was made by Randle Holme, who was deputy to the College of Arms for Cheshire. He copied it from a bond dated 1390-91 by Roger the Prior to Sir Nicholas de Audley.

Fig. 30: The Priory Seal. (Photo reproduced by permission of British Library).

Appendix IV
JOBS that had to be undertaken in ABBEYS and PRIORIES

In small Priories like Birkenhead these jobs would be amalgamated.

The Bursar would look after the accounts.

The Librarian would care for the books and run the library. ('liber' is the Latin name for book.)

The Almoner would have charge of the alms and divide them on Founder's day. He would see to bread and perhaps clothing, etc., for beggars.

The Chamberlain looked after the beds and bedding, linen, clothing, razors, towels, lamps.

The Kitchener performed the duties of a Chef and was concerned with the preparation of meals.

The Refectorian would see to the serving of meals and to the plate and table linen, etc.

The Cellarer would see to the wine and provisions. He would have charge of the cellars and storerooms and attend to everything to do with food and drink and fuel too, (wood and firing), and provisions generally. He would have duties with regard to strangers.

The Hospitaller was the guest master. 'Hospes' means 'guest'.

The Infirmarian looked after the sick monks and might be regarded as a doctor by visitors or populace nearby. (There were few hospitals and doctors.) He would grow herbs in the garden and concoct medicines and ointments. Monks in his sick ward would be allowed to eat flesh.

The Pittancer looked after 'extra' dishes called pittances. These were small allowances over and above common provisions.

The Precentor undertook the training of the choir and had charge of the music and books.

The Sacrist or Sacristan or Sexton kept the Church clean and fresh. He took care of the robes and vestments worn by the priests. He looked after valuable linen, processional banners, altar vessels, books and candles. He saw to the oblations of the great altar and to legacies. He had duties similar to those of a parish clerk. He had responsibility for burials.

The Benedictines often employed servants for jobs such as that of porter, gate-keeper, cook, gardener, scullion, swineherd, baker etc. These jobs were frequently held thoughout life and handed down from father to son.

A large Abbey would have a Lord Abbot, a Prior, a Sub-Prior, a Master of Fabrick and a Master of Novices. The job of Headmaster would apply when a school was run.

They might have writers who transcribed for the library or for the use of the house. They might also have a Circa (night watchman).

POST-SCRIPT

Birkenhead Priory was in existence during the reigns of seventeen kings. Think of the time between the Spanish Armada and our day. — From when Elizabeth I was becoming an old lady — to now. This is approximately the length of time that our Priory was in being. Many generations of men served God as monks here in Birkenhead.

Let us take ourselves back to the day that the dedication service of the Priory took place. The Bishop of Coventry and Lichfield and other dignitaries would have gathered, resplendent in colourful mitres and copes. The Abbot of Chester and the Prior of Birkenhead would be there with the monks. The priests from the churches in the Wirral would have arrived. In would stride that great Norman baron, Hamo de Mascy, with his knights and esquires, all magnificently dressed with their swords sheathed and their shining helmets carried. It must have been a glittering scene with processional banners and an altar gleaming with candles. But what was happening in the rest of the country? — England was very sparsely populated. (How astonished that foundation day congregation would be if they could come back and see the teeming millions who inhabit our country today and the sprawling urban industrialization in place of their green and wooded land.) As Hamo genuflected and knelt in the Priory church did his thoughts stray momentarily to the wars that were being waged in England between the King, Stephen, and Matilda, the daughter of the previous king, Henry I, who was the rightful heir? Perhaps he guessed that it would be Matilda's son who would reign next as Henry II. He could not know what history had in store, that the Archbishop of Canterbury, Thomas a Becket, would be murdered in his cathedral by four knights who thought they were carrying out the wishes of the king.

As the monks went about their daily business, Richard I, (the Lion-heart), succeeded his father, and the Crusades were

66

fought. Legend tells us that Robin Hood and his outlaw band were living in Sherwood Forest! Did any traveller ever relate to the monks that King John had been forced to acknowledge Magna Carta in 1215? Edward I succeeded his father, Henry III. In this reign they were certainly involved in matters of state. In 1282 our Priory had to provide carts to carry food to the king's soldiers. Edward's armies were always fighting the Welsh. The king even visited the Priory on two occasions. The first time was supposedly to receive the homage of the Welsh Prince, Llewelyn. Two years later, in 1277, came the second visit. This must have been an overwhelming occasion for the monks, and it lasted for several days. Edward came to meet the envoys of Alexander III of Scotland and of Robert de Insula, the Prince Bishop of Durham. They wanted the English king to settle a dispute about boundaries. The Bishop of Durham had accused the Scots of encroaching on his territory.[2]

Edward I was supposed to be a very striking-looking man in something of the same dashing mould as his former kinsman, Richard the Lionheart. They obviously both had a love of fighting, Richard in the Holy Land and Edward nearer to home in Wales. — Queen Eleanor accompanied the king on his visit. She stayed at Shotwick Castle. He brought his treasury and his chancery as well. What a sight it must have been as they made their way towards the Priory. Perhaps the king and his entourage would be on horseback. All the wagons and carriages would be trundling behind. Imagine feeding them all! What a task for the Priory Cellarer. A roll has survived which gives details of the sums spent each day of the king's visit.

(On 31st July, 4-shillings was offered at the altar of the church.)

For chamber and hall each day
(for coal; faggots; litter) ..	1-shilling and 8-pence respectively.
Dispensary each day	from 17-shillings to 11-shillings.
Butler	from £2.8.11d. to £1.13.9d.

Cook	from £3.9.6.d. to £2.2.7½d.
Scutler	from 8-shillings 4-pence to 6/11d.
Saucerer	from 3-shillings 11-pence to 2/6d.
Stable (for hay; corn; barley)	from £8.12.2½d. to £5.0.0d.

And it wasn't just the king's party that had to be fed, sixty-three people came for the king's alms and the monks had to feed them too.[3] This cost 7/10½d.

While Edward was at the Priory he used the Prior's barge to go up river to Stanlow. He departed in the direction of Flint.

Out of Edward's very large family, it was a pity that the son to succeed him, Edward II, was a weak character who had favourites. However, this was the king who granted the Prior's Petition for permission to erect a hostel and to charge travellers. Edward II was forced to abdicate. In 1327 he was murdered. His heir, Edward III, gave the Priory the ferry rights. During his reign, which lasted fifty years, the hundred years war against France began and famous battles, such as Crecy and Poitiers, were fought. Edward III's son, the Black Prince, died before his father. Did the fame of the battle of Agincourt ever reach Birkenhead? Much later did news of the Wars of the Roses spread to the Priory? With the demise of Richard Crookback the scene was set for the Tudors. As the monks farmed at their grange and ferried their wares to market, they could not know that the days of their Priory were now numbered. After Henry VII, a strong, able and crafty ruler, came the much-married Henry VIII, the king who, in 1536, on a day in early summer, suppressed our Priory.

As well as the beginnings of the Parliamentary system, the four hundred years of the Priory's existence saw the development of towns and the building of many of the castles and cathedrals that we enjoy visiting today. England grew rich because of the wool trade. The poor people suffered under the feudal system. For those who survived the Black Death in 1348-9, conditions began to improve. A third to a half of the

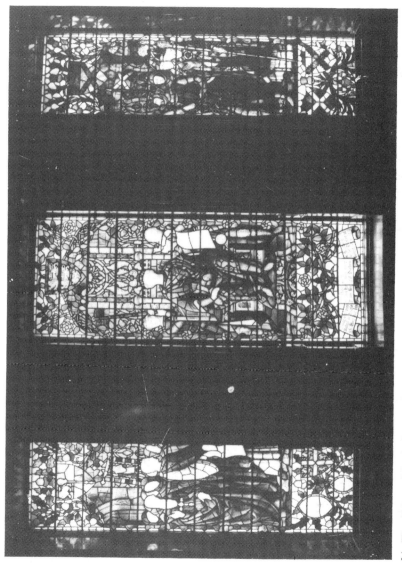

Fig. 31: The Edward 1 window on the grand staircase in Birkenhead Town Hall was designed by Gilbert P. Gamon and unveiled in July 1904. It commemorates the visit of Edward to the Priory in 1277.

population had died. Labour was scarce and the reward for it greater.

---

[1] It is possible that the Priory was founded in the reign of Henry II (1154-89) or Richard I (1189-99).

[2] When the window on the Grand Staircase in Birkenhead Town Hall came to be replaced, members of the Historic Society of Lancashire and Cheshire suggested that the replacement should commemorate the visit of Edward I to the Priory in 1277. The resulting tripartite window was designed and made by Gilber P. Gamon of London. It was unveiled in July 1904. A booklet describing the window is in Birkenhead Library.

[3] There may have been a wooden shelter for beggars outside the almonry window. An alms token, called a Nuremberg token, was found thereabouts in 1897. It had been dropped at the end of the 13th century and is now in the Williamson Museum. This early English Jetton or counter came from one of the Anglo-Gallic mints in France. The heraldic rose (for England) may have been suggested by a badge of Edward I.

BIBLIOGRAPHY

The Antiquities of England and Wales. Vol. I	*Francis Grose F.A.S.*	1773
The History of Co. Palatine and City of Chester	*Geo. Ormerod.*	1819
History of the Hundred of Wirral	*W.W. Mortimer.*	1847
History and Antiquities of Birkenhead Priory	*William I. Mason and A.W. Hunt.*	1854
Birkenhead Priory	*Charles Aldridge F.R.I.B.A.*	1887
An Account of the Benedictine Order of Monks	*Rev. Canon Linton.*	1888
The Hundred of Wirral	*Philip Sulley.*	1889
Birkenhead Priory	*Edward W. Cox.*	1894
Memories or the Chronicles of Birkenhead	*Mrs. Hilda Gamlin.*	1897
A Summary of British History	*Rev. Edgar Sanderson M.A.*	1898
History of Church and Parish of St. Mary on the Hill, Chester	*Earwaker.*	1898
Explanatory Statement — King Edward I Window	*Birkenhead Corpn.*	1904
The Beauty and Interest of Wirral	*Charles William Budden.*	1921
Priory of St. Mary and James	*Corpn. of Birkenhead.*	1923
Birkenhead Priory and the Mersey Ferry[1]	*R. Stewart-Brown.*	1925
Old Cheshire Families and their Seats	*Lionel M. Angus-Butterworth.*	1932
The Romance of Wirral	*A.G. Caton.*	1946
Old Cheshire Churches	*Raymond Richards.*	1947
Birkenhead Yesterday and Today	*W.R.S. McIntyre.*	1948
Birkenhead Priory and After	*W.F. Bushell M.A.*	1950
The Parish Church of Birkenhead and Priory Ruins	*Rev. Kenneth Lee M.A.*	1955
The Wirral Peninsula	*Norman Ellison.*	1955

Encyclopedia of the Papacy	*Hans Kuhner Ph.D.*	1959
Birkenhead Priory	*Birkenhead Corpn.*	1965
The Story of St. Benedict	*By a Benedictine of Haslemere.*	1967
Monasteries	*R.J. Unstead.*	1970
The Buildings of England, Cheshire ...	*Sir Nikolaus Pevsner and Edward Hubbard.*	1971
How they lived in a Medieval Monastery	*Stig Haden ius and Birgit Janrup.*	1978
Benedictine Yearbook. *Acting Editor:*	*Rev. Gordon Beattie O.S.B.*	1981
A Short Guide to the Buildings of Birkenhead Priory	*Birkenhead Corpn.*	
A Short Guide to the Parish Church of St. Mary the Virgin, Bowdon	*Maurice H. Ridgway B.A., F.S.A.*	
The Victoria History of the Co. of Cheshire. Vol. III	*Univ. of London Inst. of Historical Research*	1980
Dunham Massey, Cheshire	*The National Trust.*	1981
"Ampleforth Abbey" booklet.		

---

[1] The chapter by Harold Brakspear is an excellent account of the buildings.